RULES OF ENGAGEMENT

RULES OF ENGAGEMENT

A Self-Help Guide for Those Overcoming Major Personal Trauma

Scoba Rhodes

LIBRARY OF CONGRESS CONTROL NUMBER:		2013913801
ISBN:	HARDCOVER	978-1-4836-7743-9
	SOFTCOVER	978-1-4836-7742-2
	EBOOK	978-1-4836-7744-6

This book was printed in the United States of America.

Rev. date: 08/07/2013

To order additional copies of this book, contact:
Xlibris LLC
1-888-795-4274
www.Xlibris.com
Orders@Xlibris.com
138463

CONTENTS

Hello, World

Hello, world—exactly. This is my first attempt at writing a book. I have gone through a tunnel of darkness and despair and have come out the other side. I want to share the experience with others and offer advice on how I managed to not only survive but also bounce back. On November 2, 2009, I went in for a medical procedure. One year earlier, doctors discovered I had an abdominal aortic aneurysm (AAA), and it needed a stent to be installed. This was nothing new to me since I had been having aneurysms in my aorta since 2003. The first one occurred in May 2003 while I was taking an aerobics class. I was strong, fit, and was actually a certified aerobics instructor since 1994. I started teaching aerobics class while I was in the navy and helped more than a few sailors shed a few pounds and continue on in their naval careers. After receiving an honorable discharge from the navy, I kept up my pursuit of fitness instruction and became a certified aerobics instructor by the Aerobics and Fitness Association of America (AFAA). I taught for Gold's Gym in San Diego and other outfits during the next ten years. No matter where I lived, I made sure fitness was a part of my life.

After my first aneurysm in 2003, I learned that my paternal grandmother died from the same affliction and that my condition was genetic. There was nothing I could do outside of trying to maintain a good diet and healthy lifestyle, for exercising was no longer an option, except brisk walking. After my operation to have my aneurysm repaired, I thought that I was going to be fine. Unfortunately, I also thought that meant I could continue on with some of my unhealthy habits. I continued to work myself to exhaustion, to the point of me driving home in danger of falling asleep at the wheel. So, of course, I had to compensate with coffee and cigarettes, which I would justify to myself by saying it was only when I was driving and only to help me stay awake. In my mind, since

I was still walking and jogging, I thought everything was well-balanced. Well, I had my second aneurysm driving home in May 2008 while I was drinking an espresso and smoking a cigarette. It was during that operation when it was discovered I had a third aneurysm. I opted for a scheduled surgery since the possibility of it bursting while I was driving was an even scarier possibility. So in November 2009, I went in to repair my AAA for what I thought would be a six-hour procedure, and I woke up eleven days later, barely able to breathe and unable to move my legs.

The first emotion I experienced was worry that my girlfriend would no longer want me. Then I was angry at the doctor, then at myself, then at the world. I could say I experienced every negative emotion available over the next six months. I felt anger, fear, loathing, loneliness, denial, depression, sadness, helplessness, embarrassment, mistrust, paranoia, and finally, remorse. Not sure if I have completely recovered from that trauma yet, but I am coping better. This, I hope, will be one additional way of healing. You see, when I was initially injured, I lay in my bed for two months crying, without a single visit from a counselor or even a social worker. Additionally, while at the rehabilitation hospital, I had three hours a day of physical rehab and one hour a week of mental counseling.

Looking back, I think I would have benefited much more if there was some counseling before the physical working-out phase and more counseling throughout the entire process. In reference to the ancient proverb "Trying to fix the body without fixing the mind is like building a castle on shifting sand," it is my contention that mental recovery from a traumatic accident is as important as any amount of physical rehabilitation. I have found that the best therapy is to interact and converse with people in the same situation or, at least, a similar one. Healthy people, I feel (unless they are some sort of caregiver), cannot fathom the experience of waking up to find your whole world has been altered, and for the worse. There is so much I have yet to learn on how to live. Things I used to do on the spur of the moment I now must schedule ahead of time. My whole day revolves around when I must go to the bathroom, shower, get dressed, cook, and clean. I had to master those things before I could think about getting my life back in order. Actually, they are called *activities of daily living*. I felt as if I was starting my life all over again. But where was I to begin?

A Question of Faith

First of all, I must admit I have spent most of my adult life an atheist. Yes, I grew up Catholic—first communion, altar boy, and confirmation ceremony and all. I went to catechism (church instruction) for five years as well. Then when I was in college, I stopped going to church, although I started back up again when I was in the navy. After getting discharged, I stopped again. I guess you could say I went to church only when it suited me and my needs. When times were trying, I would turn to God for support. When times were going well, I would watch football on Sunday mornings. My main problem was all those rules, especially the ones concerning marriage and fidelity. You could definitely say that if there was a scorecard kept by Jesus, he would *not* be very pleased with me at all. So, I guess, rather than face that possibility of having to account for my behavior, I found it easier to say there was no one to be accountable for except myself. Thus, I discontinued my belief in God.

Now my mother turned to Buddhism when I was ten years old. You could say that I was raised Buddhist by default—or in Buddhist terms, I was a "fortune baby." I was not forced to practice that philosophy; however, I was around it so much it became very much ingrained in my consciousness. Are the two contraindicated? I don't think so. There is quite a bit of crossover between the two philosophies, but that is a discussion for another day.

I went on that way for many years, learning and practicing a Buddhist philosophy and attending various Buddhist temples until I ended up in the hospital last year hanging on for dear life. Then I found myself asking for a priest to come and give me a healing prayer. Suffice it to say, when the fat was in the fire and I thought my day of judgment might be at hand, I chose grace over karma.

How did I justify that sudden belief change, you ask? I simply called myself hedging my bets. I cannot speak for you, but I found that when I was facing death as a real possibility, I did not have as much faith in myself as I thought I did. You see, I learned karma is a great philosophy when you are healthy and the worst thing that happens to you is you trip and fall down a set of stairs. Your friends then laugh and say, "That's karma for you." But what is your feeling when you are looking death in the face and all you have to hold on to are your own deeds and misdeeds? I began to remember all the things I had done that were not so honorable, and even though no one knew about them, I knew. And not knowing where I could possibly be headed during this moment of real crisis, I began to cry out for that same God I was raised to worship and begged for forgiveness.

Now, I am still not sure I can say I believe in God, but I do believe in all that God stands for. What that means is, I do not pray to God for the gift of walking. I don't believe that is how God works. God is not there to give us our desires. He is not someone who stands above us in judgment and dishes out rewards and punishments. He is there as a higher power in order to provide us with strength and motivation to be all that we *can* be, even in the face of adversity.

Now that definition will vary from person to person, but for me, it means having the strength to carry on with the rest of my life and still excel at the things I can excel in. Yes, I can no longer walk, but that does not mean I can no longer work, play, love, help, and excel. Maybe I'll have to change careers. I'd probably need assistance with some things for the rest of my life and would need to be more careful with my skin and overall health, but my life still goes on. And it doesn't mean that I will have any less joy in it either.

At the first onset of my paralysis, I previously explained the gauntlet of emotions that I experienced. One emotion I experienced was fear. And fear was a major one. Couple that with depression and there is a disaster waiting to happen. I started talking to the priest at the VA hospital. I learned a very interesting take on the word *fear*. If you look at the word, it is made up of two interesting components. The first part is the letters *Fe*, also the symbol for iron—a cold, hard, rigid metal that stands resolute, unmoving, and unforgiving to any stress placed upon it. The second part is *Ar*, the symbol for argon—an inert gas that cannot mix with anything. It too stands alone. If you put those definitions together, you can come up with a definition that describes an unmoving, unforgiving state of existence that refuses to allow you contact with any other aspect of your life. It may sound pretty harsh, but that is exactly how I behaved during the first few months of my injury.

It took faith to bring me to the point where I am now. Not just faith in God but also faith in my friends, faith in my wife, faith in my family, faith in my medical staff, and finally, faith in myself. I needed to have faith that I could still overcome obstacles that were placed before me. Yes, I had fewer tools than before, but I still had plenty at my disposal. And I may still have some that I have yet to discover. But I have faith that I will discover them. It was this faith in my future and in myself that provided me with the strength to get out of bed every morning, to go to my therapies at the hospital, to go start looking at schools for a new education and career, to eat properly, and to be careful about losing any more ground physically.

Fear is allowing the unknown to force you to stand rigid, unmoving, and therefore unaware of all that exists in the world. Faith can give you the courage to face that unknown with determination, curiosity, excitement, and of course, love. In other words, I'd like to adjust an old proverb derived from the Bible: "Fear makes the mountain that faith can move."

Who Benefits from This Book?

If you are sitting in a hospital, staring at a missing limb, breast, or unable to move a particular part of your body, then this book is written for you. If you are suffering from a broken limb, recovering from internal surgery or facing a serious program of rehabilitation due to your injuries, then this book may be interesting, but you won't find any of these concepts applicable directly to your particular situation. Only those who have a tough road ahead of them—not only in recovering in the hospital but also in reentering their previous lifestyle and having the simultaneous challenge of accepting and understanding their new body—will find this book helpful in any sense. I do not approach my healing from a Christian, Catholic, Buddhist, Muslim, or Jewish standpoint.

I do not approach it even from a new-age spiritual standpoint. I further acknowledge that there are some of you out there who are so adept at overcoming adversity that you can and will recover from your injuries without any help from me. By the same token, there are those that no words can help, no matter where they come from. My hope is to reach the rest of you out there, the ones with so much potential to continue on and lead perfectly satisfying lives if you just get a little guidance.

The best time to receive this guidance is as soon as your brain is able to retain information. That is to say, the brain retains information better when the painkillers have been weaned down to a pain pill every four hours. The brain cannot fully function under the influence of morphine or any other mind-altering drug you may find in a hospital. That being said, you will find the doctors working hard to manage your pain level. Don't try and be a hero here. The lower your pain level, the better the body can concentrate its energies on the healing process. Eventually, the body will heal, and it will be time for rehabilitation. You may have to get used to using a prosthetic arm, leg, or two arms and legs. Or maybe you have to cope with legs that no longer move or possibly a missing breast, prostate, or colon due to cancer. Don't try to compare here. Just ask yourself, is there any body part you won't miss if you have to give it up?

So you have awakened with some part of your body missing, and maybe you have had a visit from a compassionate counselor (or maybe not). If you lost a limb in the line of duty, you have had a visit from your local Wounded Warrior chapter. The worst-case scenario is that you are left to your own devices with no advice given to you or your family, and you are left to lie paralyzed in the hospital bed, gathering bedsores, all during the Thanksgiving and Christmas holidays. You ask, is that even possible? Yes, because that was my personal experience. I share this not to compare but to impress upon you that I may have some real advice to share. When I say that I know that some of you will emotionally be at the point of despair and wondering if you should continue on with your life, it is because I too have felt the same way.

It was not until seven months into my accident, when I dropped to 175 pounds from 240, that my wife said, "I need you to take your rehab seriously. I am tired of watching you waste away into nothing. You are not the only one affected by your accident, you know."

I was up all night wondering how to move forward and get myself out of this mood of despair. The hospital was willing to provide me antidepressants, but I knew those would not work. I had all my family members and hospital staff constantly trying to cheer me up, and that still wasn't working. Then, late into the night or early the next morning, I had an epiphany and wrote down my first rule of engagement. It was that first revelation that altered my mood toward my rehabilitation and placed me on the path toward my mental recovery. See, while the hospital was wonderful at working and challenging me physically, the hospital was not very adept at helping me mentally.

Yes, a few months into the injury, I had a psychologist visit me once a week, and she monitored my mental-health state, but it was one hour a week of mental and emotional assistance and three hours a day of physical exercise. I have since come to the conclusion that the mental work should begin as soon as possible. Unfortunately, there are not too many counselors or psychologists that want to take on the emotional work required to help many trauma patients over that initial shock and through the first few months of the emotional roller coaster that accompanies someone lying in a hospital bed, trying to figure out how the rest of their life is going to look like with a limb missing. What about my job, friends, and most of all, my girlfriend or wife?

This book is written for those people who find themselves in that moment, hovering over the choice between life and death. They may not be placing a gun to their heads, but people can choose to kill themselves slowly or just live from day to day, hating the world—which is choosing to live a life that is not much worth living. I choose to look at that decision also as suicide since it is killing an opportunity at an extremely fulfilling life. Many people after a major traumatic accident that leaves one paraplegic or an amputee turn to alcohol and drugs, destroying any chance of rebuilding a career, relationship, or life. Although after some time you can bounce back, what about those lost years you can never get back? I want to save you from ever having to look back with any notions of regret. It is even quite possible to look back over your life, include the accident, and feel a sense of joy and contentment. Maybe not today or tomorrow or even this year, but one day you can. My rules are not the only paths to recovery, but if you need specific steps and actions you can do now while you are in the hospital, then this book is for you.

Rules of Engagement

Being stuck in a situation, especially after a major trauma, can make you feel as if there is no way out and that you are stuck in this situation forever. Although there is no guarantee that any method will be your salvation, I realized during my own personal experience that there are steps that can be taken that can lift most anyone out of any deep hole. These steps, however, are not any type of getting-rich formula; they are thought processes and actions you can engage in to lift you out of a situation you may find it impossible to recover from—like the loss of a limb, sudden paralysis, mastectomy, heart attack, or a multiple sclerosis (MS) or cancer diagnosis. This is not, however, a cure-all, nor is it meant to be. If you find someone is suffering from a major traumatic brain injury, these steps will be futile. There must be a cognitive mind functioning in order for any of this book to be of assistance to anyone.

OK, folks, here it is. These rules not only are applicable directly to my experience but, I hope, will also benefit anyone as you travel on this highway called life. I shall write each rule down in this first chapter. Then in subsequent chapters, I will specify each rule concerning the relevance to my experience then to the experience of *life*.

1. *You* are your first line of defense.
2. Put someone in your corner who will *not* let you fail.
3. Learn to be happy with nothing.
4. Depression? OK, but don't let it rule over you forever.
5. Life goes on, with or without you.
6. Every day, take time to play, even if it is for just a little while.

7. Don't measure yourself by what happens to you but by how you handle what happens to you.
8. Never *ever* stop dreaming.
9. Love is not the answer, but it may be the key.
10. You've got to stop and smell the roses.

You Are Your First Line of Defense

When I went in for my AAA repair, I completely trusted the doctor to perform the surgery successfully. Why not? I had two similar operations done before, which were done with success. Yes, there was some tough recovery involved accompanied with some physical therapy, but all in all, I had come out perfectly healthy. I did not think for one moment I was pushing the envelope to undergo another surgery even though, when I look back, I was warned about the dangers accompanied with this third procedure.

When I arrived at Harbor-UCLA Medical Center and spoke with the surgeon regarding my operation, I was met with reasonable assurance that there would not be any problems with my operation. Yes, there were some risks, I was told by the doctor, but the risks were small, and I should be fine. Unfortunately, that did not turn out to be the case. I woke up paralyzed, and I could not believe how this happened to me. I wanted to blame the surgeon, then the VA, then anyone else I could find. I even wanted to blame my parents for passing on this genetic trait that had made my life so difficult. Yes, folks, my parents were to blame for passing on a genetic disease to me. And for a while, I found comfort in this mode of thought.

However, while I was busy blaming the world for my condition, I was wasting away. I was not eating correctly; I was too angry at the VA kitchen. I was not working out properly; actually, I would show up fifteen to twenty minutes late and would not get a good workout in. I didn't care about anything, I couldn't care less actually, about whether my therapist showed up to my room or not, whether I ate or not, or whether the sun rose or set. And while I was wallowing in my self-pity, my wife and family were watching me slowly waste away into nothing. It wasn't until my wife said to me "I've tried everything I could to help you. I bring you healthy food, visit you almost every evening, and stay here just about every weekend. I still have to work at my job, pay rent, and buy food and gas to visit you. But all you're doing is wasting away into nothing, and I can't watch that anymore" that I did some major self-reflection that night.

I began to realize that there was more to my present situation than I was willing to admit. Truth be told, I was warned about my situation during my recovery after the first operation in 2005. I was told to stop smoking; I didn't. I was told to exercise more; I didn't. I was told to change my diet; I didn't. I was told to watch my blood pressure; I didn't. Now, did I find reasonable excuses for not following the advice of the doctors that first time? Sure. I was too busy at work, trying to climb my way up the corporate ladder. I was only smoking a few cigarettes per day and only in the car. (Ha-ha.) It was only pizza and beer on the weekends, so that was OK, and so on. But I didn't learn my lesson, and in May 2008, I had another aneurysm burst while I was driving on the freeway. This one I barely survived, but as I look back, there is one memory that I am loath to admit. When this occurred, I was driving while smoking a cigarette and drinking espresso. Was this directly responsible for the aneurysm burst? I will never know. But I can say for sure that it did not *help* the situation.

The point to realize here is that I was looking at and understanding the role I played in arriving at my present situation, not to try to blame myself or to play the martyr but to realize that I do have some measure of power over my own present and future. You see, I learned a long time ago that if you blame others for your situation, you are essentially giving others power over your life. However, when I was in the pit of depression, I could not see what I was doing until I took that long look at myself. By understanding what role I played in my situation, I was essentially returning some measure of power back to myself, and then I was able to find the energy to get myself out of it. But I was smart enough to know that it would take more than just one little revelation. I was going to need some real help to overcome my depression and newfound disability. This was a major change in my life, and it was going to take a major plan to adjust to it.

It was then I realized I was going to need a step-by-step process designed to get me out of this downward spiral. My family, nurses, and even psychologist tried to help me, but when you are in that pit of despair—and there is no getting around this—you need a step-by-step process to get you out of it. Others try, but in doing so, they make it worse. You hear words like "Everything's going to be OK, try and cheer up, you can do this, and I understand how you must feel, blah, blah." Believe me, I heard them all too. What I learned during that time was that my recovery was going to need to be accomplished in steps if it was going to be successful. You will notice in my rules, dealing with the depression doesn't even happen until step four. But the first three steps really need to occur before you can successfully cope with your depression. This I also learned from being there.

So now I am in a wheelchair, but I am looking at life in a very different way. I do not touch cigarettes, I haven't had a pizza in over a year, I eat oatmeal at least once a week for breakfast, and I take my medication every single day and try to keep up my vitamins and supplements. Am I perfect? I would have to answer *no*. Am I a whole world better than I was? I would have to answer *absolutely*. The problem was that I had to lose the use of my legs to finally get the message. Understand, I am not blaming myself for my condition, and I am not wallowing in self-pity. But I do believe that in any instance that occurs to us, we have the responsibility to ask ourselves what role we played in arriving at our situation. If we can do that, we can also play a role in improving our situation and possibly prevent it from becoming worse. The reason for this is because once we take responsibility for our situation in life, we also gain power over our situation. And once we gain power over our situation, we then can begin to change that position. I am not saying that we can grow a limb or become able-bodied, but we can begin to affect change in our mood, then in our rehabilitation, and eventually, in our lives.

When we wake up each morning, I now believe we need to make a commitment to ourselves to ensure that our day and our life will be as healthy and productive as possible. When we end up in the hospital for any reason, we should ask ourselves, what role did we play in landing ourselves there? Was there someone's advice that we did not follow? Did we eat something we should not have? And before we decide to be rude to a caregiver, nurse, doctor, or volunteer, we should ask ourselves, were we as clear as we could have been in our questions? Have we been as friendly as we could have been to the staff? Is this something I could really do myself and I just want someone to do it for me? Yes, I realize you have just been dealt a terrible blow, but remember, the doctors are here to help you, and the sooner you can get your head in the game, the better off your future will be.

Realize, I am not saying that we are to blame for everything that happens to us, and most certainly, we can be the victim of an incident of which we have no control over. I am only asking, what was the part we played in arriving at our present situation? Were we responsible in some way for our condition? And what can *we* do to ensure our day goes as smoothly as it could possibly go? We must be aware that we are our first line of defense, and that means taking responsibility for ourselves, thus giving ourselves the power to shape, at least in part, the remainder of our lives.

Put Someone in Your Corner Who Will *Not* Let You Fail

Some of the most vivid memories I have of my difficult recovery from my accident were the two times the doctors attempted to wean me off the CPAP machine or otherwise called a breathing apparatus. The first attempt failed, and within a few hours, I was back on the breathing machine. I was still too weak to breathe on my own. I can't say I remember that since I was unconscious the first time. However, the second time I remember vividly because I was conscious when my breathing was failing again, and I had to again be placed on the breathing machine. If not for Sonia (my then girlfriend) standing by me, instructing me to breathe deeply, all the while smiling to me, trying to keep me calm, I most likely would not have made it through that experience. However, that is not the event to which I am referring.

My father and Sonia were told that the third time they removed the breathing apparatus, I would not be placed back on it. If I was not able to breathe on my own, then they were going to remove all life support. I did not know this at the time, but those were the circumstances. This was because prior to my operation, I signed a form (code orders) stating I did not want to be left on breathing assistance for an extended period of time. I now have changed that belief.

So the breathing machine was removed, and I commenced to attempt to breathe on my own. This was the absolutely hardest thing I ever had to do. I could barely move my lungs, and every breath felt like it took all my energy to complete. Time was moving at a snail's pace. My perception was that an hour had passed, but then I would glance at the clock and see only fifteen minutes had actually passed. This was supreme agony for me, and while my father and Sonia were diligently taking turns watching over me, encouraging me, keeping me breathing, I found myself running out of energy. It was during one of Sonia's turns that I did not want her to see me in such a weak state as I was about to make a very difficult request. I asked her to go and get my father, and at first she asked me why then thought better of it and went and got him for me. I asked my father to get me placed back on the breathing machine because I could not continue. Deep within me I realized I was essentially committing suicide, but I truly felt that my days had ended and I was not going to make it.

Without even thinking, he said no. I told him I could not continue, and he simply said I could and I *would*. I just needed to take it one breath at a time. He saw me looking at the clock, so he pulled the curtain so I could no longer see it. I kept on breathing simply because I had no other option. It hurt too much to simply stop, because at some point, I would need to take a breath or I would begin to pass out. Besides, he or Sonia would just yell at me until I started breathing again. Then they switched places, and Sonia came in and made it clear that I was not going to get rid of her again and I had to keep breathing just like my father made me. My lungs felt as if they were on fire and filled with liquid. Each breath took so much energy and strength; I truly felt that I could not take another breath and that each would be my last. Sonia and my dad kept on pushing me, telling me I could do it, to not give up, and that they were right beside me. I resigned myself to simply concentrating on breathing, and eventually, it began to get easier. My lungs began to clear a bit. It wasn't much, but I could feel my lungs able to take in a bit more oxygen.

My father and Sonia kept taking turns, and eventually, my lungs became stronger. Finally, it seemed that I was going to be able to make it through this, and my father pulled back the curtain. When I glanced at the clock, I was shocked to see that almost eight hours had passed. I could not believe it, and additionally, I could not have done this on my own. If I was alone or with people other than my Dad or Sonia, I would have failed in this task and died.

I wonder how many times I gave up on something in my life before this. I remember being placed with a challenge in high school, and I shirked away from it. I attended a private school in my junior year, and my grades were not passing in chemistry. I did not get along with some teachers and got busted for attempting to purchase alcohol from a local beer-and-wine store. Over the summer, I received a letter from the school, stating that in order for me to return to the school, I would need to submit a letter to the dean of students, stating the reasons I should be allowed back for my senior year and what behavior changes I would make to increase my performance at the school. My father opted to send me back to my hometown public school and not let me return to the private school. I allowed that to happen, and even though I was just a child, as I look back, I should have noticed that a pattern was beginning to take shape.

Again I was placed with a challenge when it was time to go to college. I was provided the opportunity to apply to an Ivy League school and also one of the military academies. I chose not to face the college that was ripe with challenge and adversity and consequently picked the school I thought would be easier. Additionally, while I was there, I shied away from the sciences and chose the humanities, not because I had a passion for it but because, again, I thought it would be easier.

I was placed with a major challenge when I first joined the navy, and again, I did not rise up to the task. I was given a commission into the United States Navy, but during Officer Candidate School, I became afraid and convinced myself that I did not want to be a supply officer, so I left. Soon after that, I realized I needed to stop that pattern of quitting and failure, so I returned to the navy recruiter and reenlisted and attended the Nuclear Power School. This time, this was what I wanted to do, and I refused to be intimidated by the challenge and ended up having a successful career in the navy. I was the battle station reactor operator, was involved in a major evacuation of an erupting volcano, fought in Desert Storm, and earned various ribbons, medals, and a Letter of Commendation from the Admiral in 1991 for my efforts.

Now did I have someone in my corner those times? No, not like the ones I have today. There are those who believe you should be able to make your own decisions and allow you to do so. And there are some that may not agree with your decisions and, therefore, do not support you as vigorously as they could. I guess many people these days prefer to mind their own business and let you make whatever decisions you will make. That is OK if you have perfect decision-making capacity. However, now that I look back, I think it is a far better friend, girlfriend, family member, or wife when he/she is by your side and does not allow you to give up on your decisions, aspirations, or dreams. They are yours, and you need to have someone by your side that is willing to ensure that you obtain them. Of course, taking this approach may mean that your supporter will initiate actions that you do not enjoy. It may mean waking you up and dragging you to the gym when you would rather be asleep. It may be refusing to allow you to go to Jack in the Box or to the closest Starbucks when you have asked for help in losing that last twenty pounds. Maybe it is the person who tells you to get to the nearest VA hospital and have the doctor look at what may be a new pressure ulcer that may be forming.

These are the folks who will point out situations to you without fear of your reaction. Your anger, fear, or embarrassment takes second place to your health and vitality. Maybe these are the types of people who can spur us onto greater levels of achievement in spite of the odds we are facing due to whatever physical disability we have. It is during those times that you want someone in your corner that will go to any length to keep you on track, not by doing it for you but by giving you the support that you need to keep going. Sometimes that support may not be friendly, but maybe, being too friendly was not doing the job. Maybe we need a hard kick in the ass. A real friend will give you that when you need it. Remember, support doesn't always look like what we want it to look like, but it is still support nonetheless. This is the type of person you need in your corner while you are recovering from your accident and getting ready to enter into your rehabilitation program.

Learn to Be Happy with Nothing

Yeah, right! This is probably what most of you reading this are thinking right about now. But this is not just some random thought pulled out of thin air. When I had lost the use of my legs, I had experienced what most doctors would call a major trauma. This was not only due to a loss of a major body part but also due to a major change of lifestyle that I had to get used to. Eventually, I had to ask myself, why was this such a major loss to me? I mean, of course, I felt a loss; any normal person would. But the question I needed an answer to was, Why did it hurt me so and fill me with so much fear and anger?

I began to remember a self-taught lesson by a hero of mine, one of our founding fathers, Benjamin Franklin. While he was still printing his paper, the *Pennsylvania Gazette*, he was chastised by a local politician who had threatened him to retract a statement or face possible financial ruin. His initial response was one of fear, but his solution helped me get through my situation quite well. His solution was to eat only porridge for breakfast, lunch, and dinner. He also slept on the floor for the entire month, with all the windows open. What he learned was that even if someone took all his money and all he could afford was porridge, and if someone took all his furniture and he had to sleep on the floor, he would still survive to write another day. What this did for him was provide him with the confidence to stand up to anyone who tried to tell him what to print in his newspaper—not because he realized he was stronger than those who would try to control him, but because even if others successfully followed through on their threats against him, he would still survive their worst onslaught.

Now I did not actually go through all those exercises, but I did spend some time with some quadriplegics, folks who did not have the use of their arms *and* their legs (yes, I know you guys know what it means). I found their attitudes very optimistic toward life and their future. If they could be happy without their arms and legs, why couldn't I be happy without just my legs? I saw patients inside and outside of the hospital who were worse off than I was physically, but they were happy. They were enjoying themselves at sporting events and learning how to rock-climb and swim and play soccer, volleyball, and basketball—modified for wheelchairs and disabled people, obviously, but the point was that they were participating and having a great time.

I have since encountered fully able-bodied people, with the full use of both arms and legs, who were in the most miserable of moods. I am sure they had some issue that was weighing heavily on their minds, but they felt the desire to take it out on whoever was closest to them. But after seeing a group of people who lived every minute of every day being unable to run, jump, or throw (some unable to feed themselves) and yet spreading sunshine with their smiles and attitudes, I learned that adversity was a part of life. Everyone goes through it in some way or another, and some go through so much more than others. However, fear and anger are choices that we make, and we can choose to be afraid and angry just as easily as we can choose to be courageous and cheerful.

Whatever the situation or adversity, we can meet it with courage and cheer. When I say the outcome will reap greater rewards, I am talking from experience. But to be real, I am not saying that positive thinking will bring you the best results possible. What I am saying is that it will definitely bring you better results than negative thinking will. But how can you begin to think positively, lying in this hospital bed, unable to move or walk?

What I basically did was take an inventory of my entire life. I had done this before in many self-help books, but what I did different this time was count the limbs in my body as part of the inventory. I counted my family, friends, wife, mind, possibilities, and also limbs, internal organs, everything. I found that I could stand to lose quite a whole lot more in my life and still be happy as long as I still had my heart, soul, and of course, my wife. I learned that you can never truly know how you will feel during a crisis until you have been there. Before my accident, I would look at a man in a wheelchair and become extremely thankful that it was not me in the chair. When I became faced with the prospect of it actually being me, I was not sure I could handle that change in my life. What actually transpired, though, was I was able to experience not only happiness but joy and contentment as well.

I am not saying I have accepted the thought I no longer have my legs, but I have made my peace with it. What does that mean? I think it means that I will always have hope that I will eventually walk again. But in the meantime, that does not mean that I should not enjoy everything *else* that my life has to offer. So I am working on getting my arms, shoulders, and back as strong as possible. I will participate in events that I can do in my wheelchair, and I will continue to love my wife, my family, and my friends. There are lines in a song I listen to quite often (by Keb' Mo' if you are interested):

> *Ain't got no money, nowhere to sleep*
> *Ain't got no family, no bread no meat.*
> *Ain't got no rhythm, ain't got no rhyme.*
> *Ain't getting no younger, and I'm running out of time.*

Even though he describes his situation to be as low as possible, he still cheers up later on in the song saying that as long as he has his heart and soul, he has everything he needs. Please understand, I am not saying how anyone *should* feel regarding their situation. If someone approached me that way, I would probably try to flatten their wheelchair tires. But I have been asked by a few folks how I was able to turn my attitude around. I guess, maybe, I may have been a little grumpy during my initial stay here at the VA Medical Center. I think the easiest way to describe it is that I stopped thinking of my situation as an end to my life as it used to be but as a beginning to the rest of my life. And the best way for me to make this situation work is by being happy at ground zero, so to speak.

First, it took me realizing that I needed to stop complaining about my condition since all I was doing was annoying those who were worse off than I. Then I stopped lamenting about the old friends who stopped talking to me and learned to enjoy the company of the new friends I had made here in the hospital. Instead of being angry about not being able to continue on in my career, I focused on finding a new career I could be passionate about. I used to complain about all the people I used to see hanging around the hospital. Now, I have come to realize that by embracing the friendships I have gained while staying here, being at the hospital can actually be quite fun.

There is another famous saying; actually, it comes from the first line of a poem called "Solitude" by Louisa May Alcott. It says, "Laugh, and the world laughs with you. Weep, and you weep alone. For the sad old earth must borrow its mirth, but has troubles enough of its own."

I realized basically that this means everybody has some sort of s—that they have to deal with and really do not want to hear more of mine. This does not mean that they do not care, but be careful who you complain to. (Yes, I know I ended that sentence with a preposition. Get over it.) It is quite possible that while I am complaining that I ended up a paraplegic after my operation, I am talking to someone whose relative died from an operation. So I learned to be happy I am still alive. That is what I mean.

I am not saying to be happy *with* nothing. I am saying that before *nothing* happens for the day, before *nothing* is given to you, before *nothing* is said to you—you can choose to be happy. And if you can manage to be happy at that moment, imagine the joys the rest of the day can bring. I know life is not always a bunch of roses, but then again, it is not all thorns either. We can choose which part of life we let affect us. I am working on enjoying as much of it as I can, and when it is not going so well, I am learning to roll with the punches, so to speak.

Depression? OK, but Don't Let It Rule Over You Forever

I had to think a lot about this chapter before I decided to write about it. I realize I am not a doctor, psychologist, mental-health professional, or anything remotely connected to the medical industry. I am coming to you the only way I can, and that is as a man who has experienced loss. I thought about going over my experience here, but I have done that thoroughly enough, I believe. What I am here to talk about is how to deal with the depression in *your* life by explaining how I dealt with it in mine.

Do I know every experience is different? Yes. Do I know that no one can speak for another? Yes. Do I accept that everyone taking antidepressants cannot help the situations they are in? No. Nope. Nada. *Nicht.* Uh-uh. I do not want to hear "But my life is different . . ." from anyone ever again. I was speaking to a woman going through remission after surviving breast cancer and dealing with having breast surgery after previously having one removed. When I asked why she was taking antidepressant medication, since after the surgery, her breasts now looked fine, she responded, "Well, you don't understand what it is like—having lost a part of your body." I decided to let that remark go at the time. Really? Then I realized that it was possible for a person to look at someone in a wheelchair and still think their problems were worse than the others. Am I saying that losing your legs is worse than losing your breast? No. However, I do not think it is a stretch to say that if the technology were such that I could undergo a surgery and install manufactured legs to replace my now-defunct ones, I would undergo it in a minute. And after I would be walking again, I believe I would feel *elated*. I would be jumping for joy, screaming at the heavens, not taking Prozac because I was still upset about losing them in the first place. Am I different? Yes.

Does that mean I don't have a voice? No. I am not judging those who take the medications. I am putting this out there to those who wish they had another way of dealing with their depression.

I was prescribed Prozac to help me with my depression. I took it for weeks and felt no improvement. I felt a little numb after a while but not happier. I thought about this and tried to figure out why. I heard the nurses call the pill "mood elevators," but my mood was not being elevated. Then I thought about the phrase "Happiness comes from within." At no point in my life did this mean more to me than at that point. If happiness came from within, how in the world would a pill give it to me? So I had to find the source of my depression and somehow expel it from me. Well, I thought the answer was obvious. The source of my depression was the fact that my legs no longer worked. So, since they would never work, was I doomed to be depressed forever? I had to look at this situation deeper, much deeper, if I were going to function in this world ever again.

After days of introspection and conversations with my psychologist, wife, family, and believe it or not, a medical assistant named T. J. (who was instrumental in my mental recovery but probably does not know it), I came to a realization. It was not the loss of my legs that depressed me but my *feelings* about the loss of my legs. This is a deep thought here, but stick with me. I had to realize that there was no inherent significance to the existence of my legs. There are people born without body parts all the time, and they are able to function perfectly well. Why? Well, if they never had the body part to begin with, they wouldn't miss something they never had. They are not bound by the emotional loss; they simply go right to the physical training on how to function fully with the body parts that they do have. This is not to say that they don't have any emotions at all about the situation they are in.

I attended a disability-sports expo some time back, and I wrote about the experience. I had a few conversations with some of the other athletes, and I asked them if they could talk about how they felt about their disabilities. One girl immediately responded with "It is not a disability, it is a challenge." Now I am paraphrasing, but she continued with saying that everyone had challenges in their life. For some, it might be an anger problem; for some, it is emotional abuse from a parent; and for some, it is a physical issue. Now admittedly, it might seem at first that some are more difficult to overcome than others, but is that truly so? Does it have to be true that the one suffering from dyslexia is happier than the one suffering from spina bifida? It may seem so on the surface, but what if the dyslexic man is consistently blaming the world for his disability and, therefore, is angry all the time and can't keep friends or a job or a mate while the SB man copes, works out, and therefore, gets around, has a great attitude, great job, wife, and family? Even though he is using crutches and a wheelchair, he is much happier than the other guy.

Now, do I feel envious from time to time when I look at other able-bodied people? Yes. But sometimes I also laugh when I see someone upset over someone bumping into them or yelling at a cashier over a fifty-cent mistake in their bill or when I see someone completely overweight complaining about how hot it is outside. Here, I need a wheelchair for the rest of my life, and I would kill for the worst of my problems to be a situation with a cashier one day, and yet, I can be happy when this person can't. Who, then, is the disabled one? Interesting question, I had to admit. Talk about food for thought.

It was a completely different mode of thinking. Then it hit me. Mode of thinking . . . paradigm? Different mode of thinking . . . paradigm shift? I knew these terms but to actually perform it? Then, and I swear this to be true, I remembered a line from one of my favorite movies, *The Matrix*. I had a vision of Laurence Fishburne, a.k.a. Morpheus, saying to me, "Scoba. (That's me.) When are you going to learn there is a difference between knowing the path and walking the path?" "WOAH!" I said. Then the decision came. I stopped taking the Prozac. The nurses tried to get me to take it. I refused. The doctors tried to get me to take it. I refused. My inner self tried to get me to take it. I *refused!* I got up every day. I exercised every day. I attacked the weights. I ate the oatmeal my wife gave me. But most importantly, I started smiling at my assistants. Then I started telling jokes. Then I started laughing. Then I felt happy. Did I feel happy *all* the time? No. But when I came down, I learned not to *stay* down. Now it is a year and a half later, and I still am not taking Prozac, and I can say I am still happy.

I still do not walk, but the wheelchair is OK. My arms are strong, and I can get around. Yesterday my wife and I went to the beach for the first time since my injury. We had a marvelous time. We had dinner at this awesome restaurant and finished the meal with the most delicious chocolate-chip cookies I have ever had in my life. Was the food *really* that good, or was it just my attitude at the time? Who *cares*? The fact is, I am asking you to take a look at your situation and find the root of your depression. If you have all your arms and legs and your mind is intact, it may very well be possible for you to stop spending money, making billionaires out of people who are not making a product that truly benefits you in any way.

There are many people out there who will tell you that those pills you are taking are helping you. I would suggest that may not be the case. You may be missing out on some really wonderful things about life. My wife and I are having a wonderful time together. As a matter of fact, she is trying to get me off the computer right now so we can get ready and go out for a champagne brunch with her best friend and meet her new boyfriend. Is your prescription allowing you to do something like that this morning? If not, I would suggest you give my method a try. It is not something new or even complicated. It is just a search for the truth. Maybe that is what this experience is all about. Good luck. I truly mean it, my friends. To all of you, love and peace.

Life Goes On . . . With or Without You

You want a life lesson? Take this one on for size. Just in case anyone reading this is not familiar with the five stages of loss/grief, here they are: denial, anger, bargaining, despair, acceptance. I am more than confident everyone reading this will be, at least, familiar with these stages, and I'm pretty sure all have even been through them in one form or another. Even I have experienced these stages the first time I lost a family member, girlfriend, even a job. It is safe to say that almost everyone has gone through these stages for one reason or another. However, I am about to share with you my experience with these five stages as I dealt with my entire life. I would like to warn any family members, caregivers, therapists, or friends who may be reading this. If, at any time, you find it difficult to continue, please do not stop reading this section until the end. Remember, I said I was dealing with my entire life during this experience, and you would be naive to think you are not a part of it, no matter how far back in time we may travel.

Prior to and including the first few months after November 2, 2009, the day of my operation, I was in the first stage—denial. Now, I realize that there is no rule that says you have to experience the stages mentioned above in the order that I listed them, but it seems to me that denial would be the first stage of experience for most people. That would include me. I remember not being at all concerned about the operation even though both my parents and Sonia seemed, in my eyes anyway, way too concerned about this. I felt I was the calming influence here. Looking back (you may insert your favorite cliché here), I see now I was simply in the denial stage, and everyone, and I mean *everyone*, close to me was very concerned about this procedure. When I say *concerned*, both my mother and Sonia had shed tears at different times in relation to this procedure—Sonia, when it was first scheduled and my mother, the day before I checked in to the hospital. And my reaction to both? Annoyance. And I kid you not.

Anyone connected to me on the social media networks may or may not remember me posting the information of my procedure, including the dates and location of the hospital. Believe it or not, I was expecting quite a few visitors, cards, and letters to be pouring in while I was in recovery. I knew many people locally, and I figured some of them would be in to visit me. I was actually concerned that I would have too many female visitors and Sonia would become jealous and I would have to deal with that. I was truly preparing for a vacationesque period in the hospital. In a way, I was actually looking forward to it. Yes, I figured there would be some recovery and physical therapy involved but no more than the other two surgeries required. I was all set for my time in the hospital.

Now imagine my response to when I first opened my eyes. By this I mean the first time I could *remember* opening my eyes. You see, during the time I could remember opening my eyes, my hands were tied to the bed rails. I was not told why until later. As I understand it, when I first came out of the anesthesia, it was explained to me that there was an emergency and, unfortunately, I was paralyzed and I would no longer walk again. My response to this news was to attempt to rip out the lines going into my neck and "walk" out of the hospital. For those that need help keeping up here, I now refer you to the first stage of loss. During the first few weeks, the hospital helps you stay in the denial stage although here, it is considered a good thing. For if I had known my actual state of health and the real danger I was in, fear would have set in, and I would have had a much more difficult time dealing with my situation. So I was awake, and all visitors were told to just go along with anything I was saying. I remember talking about needing to get back to work as I was a bodyguard for Michael Jackson, taking strolls along different shopping malls with Sonia, experiencing a period in Jamaica with Shaquille O'Neal and Jessica Simpson, and even developing a CD-distribution firm with Will Smith. Now today's date is September 17, 2011, and I can still vividly remember these hallucinations that were taking place during November 2009. That is how powerful the feeling of denial can be. And at the time, it may have saved my life.

As my mind began to clear, I began immediately to enter into the bargaining stage. I would begin to ask for water, which I was denied. However, I would ask for ice chips, and a few were allowed each hour. No family members were allowed to stay with me after hours. Remember those hallucinations I spoke about above? Not all of them were pleasant. I was also convinced that there were vampires about in the evening and there was a conspiracy to sell my organs on the black market and my father was involved. Anyway, I refused to undergo a procedure, which I was told was important for me, unless Sonia was allowed to spend all night with me. This was more than a little upsetting to the night nurses, but I held fast. As I started to get a hold of the world around me, I started to bargain with my friends and family. There was not anywhere near the amount of support I was expecting. Yes, I had visits from my family. But other than my father, mother, brother, and sisters and Sonia, there was, maybe, one visit from other family members. Sometimes there were three or four. But I was expecting daily visits from *somebody*, and that was not occurring. Soon my sister volunteered to update my Facebook page regularly as I was convinced that, maybe, if my extended-family members' friends knew what I was going through, they would come to my rescue. Believe it or not, some did. To this day, I will remember the home-cooked meals from Suzanne, the home-baked cookies from Angel, the endless amount of food prepared for me by Gloria, the frequent calls from Leslie, and all the written communication from Kelley and Elena. My father stayed with me all day every day while he was here, and that was for more than a month. He had to return home, but he was to return two more times and rented a room in the hospital and stayed with me for weeks at a time. The nurses and doctors who cared for me all thought that my dad lived in California. They were shocked to actually learn he lived in Massachusetts. During the month of December, my brother and Sonia took turns staying the night with me, helping me deal with the shock and loneliness of my situation. But as you can see, I can remember each name of the family member or friend who stuck out the time with me in the hospital, and I can count who they were on both hands and toes.

I began texting my friends, letting them know I was still in the hospital. I would even call them on the phone, being careful not to beg, letting them know of my situation. My friends from out of state I naturally gave a pass to. But you should know that one came from southern Mexico and one came from Wisconsin to visit me. And the one from Mexico came twice. But the visits still came from the same folks and even began to drop off as I was transferred to the rehab hospital. Enter the anger stage.

No one was safe. I would question every decision my doctors made even if I agreed. I was angry at all doctors. I would argue about taking my medications with the nurses even though I knew I needed them. Sometimes I would argue about taking them while they were in the room, then wait until they left, and then I would just take them. Some of them realized what I was going through and did not take it personally and even found a way to get me to take them without any difficulty. Whatever my therapists told me to do, I complained about it, and I refused to work hard. I would rather whine and argue with everyone around me and just be as angry and bitter as I could possibly be. I realize now that I know many patients who are still in this stage. I was also angry at all local friends who did not bother to visit me, all family members who did not visit me, and all friends far and away who did not call. Why not? They knew where I was and what had happened. What was the deal? Then I would read a post a friend would make: "I had a bad day," "It is raining outside," "I am getting a cold," and I would get infuriated. The therapists even considered taking away the computer from me, thinking the news of the outside world was not conducive to my healing process. It was Dina, my wonderful psychologist, that went to bat for me here. She believed correctly that I would work through this and come to terms with the situation.

Here is the kicker. In order to get to acceptance, you have to go through despair. I wish this were not the case, and many folks with degrees will disagree. So what? Those that think they are OK and in the acceptance stage are not really there if they have not passed through despair. They are effectively in another form of denial. And I see it in people today. Acceptance is not giving up to the paralysis, hanging out at a rehab hospital, complaining about the issues of the day, or collecting government paychecks. You need to come to a sort of peace with the situation and rejoin the world and get back out there.

But the despair stage is a real bitch. I chose to go through it, and had it not been for the love of a beautiful woman, I would not have made it through as well as I did. I wanted to lash out at all who spurned me, ignored me, and left me alone in that horrible place. I lost a lot of weight and was at the skinniest as I had ever been. That was the period I would like to call the Prozac period. I have already explained how I got through that in an earlier blog, but now you have it in another context. As I worked my way through that fog, I learned a few things.

One, everyone has their own life to live, complete with their own struggles, obstacles, and triumphs. It is not the responsibility of the world to stop moving and wait for me to rejoin it. It is my responsibility to get healthy and rejoin the world. And yes, if I had not gone through *all* the stages of loss, I would not have come to the place where I am now. Am I saying everyone goes through all these stages? No, and maybe you are not either. But you may very well be experiencing one or two, and if that is the case, I hope this chapter provides you some insight on how to facilitate your own process of healing.

Nevertheless, here I am, not a happier man but a better one. I may not have control of my legs, but I am in charge of my own soul. One of my most favorite quotations is by Leo Tolstoy: "Everything I understand, I understand only because I love." (There is more if you want to check it out.) So I understand my friends because I love them. I understand my family because I love them. And I so understand the world because I love it. And I love the world because of one woman who has loved me more than I believed to be possible. And I would not have known that had I not had to walk the path of the past two years.

Every Day, Take Time to Play

Open your next *Reader's Digest* magazine. In there you will find a column that has been running for over fifty years titled "Laughter, the Best Medicine." One of my favorite authors, Mark Victor Hansen, has a series of books presenting humorous and uplifting tales sent in from people all over the world. The title of these books is *Chicken Soup for the Soul.* In the movie *Patch Adams,* Robin Williams played a doctor who believed that by making his patients laugh, he could provide some therapeutic service to them. He also did this in real life for one of his best friends. (Hint: he used to wear blue tights on the big screen.)

I'm paraphrasing here, and I hope the meaning is not lost. "Do you love life? Then do not squander time. For that's what life is made of." These words were immortalized by one of my favorite founding fathers, Benjamin Franklin. Now, there are those out there that would like to say that fun time, or recreation for that matter, is another word for wasting time. I could not disagree more. In fact, I submit that if more people recognized the importance of good, quality recreation, a lot of ills in this world would cease to exist. Certainly, you don't have to explain that concept to the NFL, NBA, or my favorite, the National League of Baseball. Why, just drive around your hometown on any Saturday morning and you might see the fields full of children and young adults playing some game or another, with parents and other family members on the sidelines, yelling and cheering. Some may also be cooking hot dogs, some drinking sodas, but if you were to ask, none would tell you that they were wasting time. Now, sitting on a couch, lying in bed, feeling sorry for yourself, complaining about how bad a hand you've just been dealt while doing absolutely nothing about it? Now, that's wasting time. And believe me, I know.

It comes as no surprise to me that having fun or recreation is a part of my life-crises advice. Why? Maybe I have learned what the people above knew all along. You may also find many doctors writing about the importance of recreation during a person's physical rehabilitation phase after a major accident or trauma. However, I have only seen the VA actually implement this. This is not to say that other rehabilitation facilities do not have this component but to say that I have not seen it. And to be honest, I have only been to two other facilities. I mean, yes, there is a recreation room, but that is not the same. What I am talking about is actual playtime—fun, interactive enjoyment. Yes, I enjoy the chess, backgammon, scrabble, and other board games, but those are saved for rainy days or recuperation times. Also, they may be good methods of introducing the recreational concept to yourself if you are weary of it.

But after a while, I recommend you getting outside for some real fun. Me? I *love* going to my nephews' football and soccer games, seeing the latest superhero movie, watching the Anaheim Angels fight their way to a World Series opportunity, hitting a sports bar when the New England Patriots are playing, or just heading out to a restaurant for a great steak or my favorite cioppino. I did all those things before my accident, and I have come to the realization that my wheelchair need not prevent me from still doing it. And of course, do not forget sex. But I have saved that for a whole other essay. The Paralyzed Veterans of America even sponsor an annual event called the National Veterans Wheelchair Games. I think, to sponsor newly injured veterans to this event is a major indicator of the belief in the importance of playtime in our lives. Although they call it recreational therapy, I believe it is to ease the placement of the idea into the nontherapeutic population. But if you are still not convinced, ask your nearest therapist, of any persuasion, just how important is recreation in our lives?

What I learned is simple. Life is meant to be enjoyed. First and foremost, when I look at people who are so driven that they value achievement above all else, I see people with a lot of money and power, but when you remove that, there does not seem to be much else. You actually find many of these people divorced, with legal troubles, unhappy family members, and completely unable to deal with a personal crisis. Although I find that many are able to justify initiating a crisis with no problem. The biggest example here is all the war we have undergone as a planet since the human race began to call itself "civilized." Further exploration of this phenomenon will require another essay. Maybe one day I will look into this. It sure would make a great thesis one day. For example, one could perform a study where someone could have sex with seventy-two women *before* going to war and then recheck and see if that person *still* wanted to kill someone. I should stop here.

As I noted in a previous essay, it is quite possible that during this crisis, you may become depressed. The doctors may quite possibly prescribe antidepressant medication. It is during this time that you must find the time to have some fun. Yeah, right, you say. So did I. But I was dragged out to sushi, barbecue, burgers, and ball games by one therapist. I was forced to go out to a restaurant, go shopping, and cook a meal by another. My favorite food was brought by my wife, and I was even delivered takeout by other folks. Heck, at my hospital, you can even get sushi or pizza delivered to your room. Yeah, it may drive your nutritionist crazy, but just learn to keep all these things in moderation. Along with this, a proper diet must be maintained. Get your fiber, vegetables, protein, and vitamins. Drink enough water each day. Read about your condition and related issues. But along with that, grab a pizza with some friends, catch a Spider-Man flick, take part in the games of the children in your family—if not your sons and daughters, then your nieces and nephews.

When you awoke from your accident or surgery, you found that your life had changed forever. You need to understand that. It wasn't "Your life is about to change or going to change." It was not "Would you like your life to change?" It was "Your life has changed." Now you have to deal with it. You may think your life has changed for the worse; you may even think it might be over as you know it. I would like to submit to you to just work through everything one step at a time. There are many facets of rebuilding your life that you may not have even seen yet. However, in the midst of all this shit that is going on, remember one thing along with everything else. That is that every day, take time to play even if it is for just a little while. I promise you, in the midst of all that is happening right now, it is possible to find a reason to smile and to laugh. And it is the best medicine.

Do Not Judge Yourself by What Happens to You

I realize this statement goes against the popular mystic theory of the law of attraction. This states that whatever you think about, subconsciously or consciously, will come to you in one form or another. I do not believe that. I have found that the notions of fate and karma only serve to remove accountability from the equation of life. However, contrary to opinions of some speakers who believe that everything in life is a result of consequence and action, I am not saying that we are responsible for everything that happens to us either. Life just is not an either-or proposition. There are things in life that we can control, and there are things in life that are beyond our control. The question we should be asking ourselves is not how we can control our environment but how we can control ourselves, especially when our environments are not cooperative with our desires. It's easy to enjoy life when life is good although some people still find it hard to do. How is it possible to enjoy life when life is not so good? Therein lies the mystery.

I can understand the difficulty in finding happiness if you have a life filled with physical pain, a lasting disability, drug abuse, divorce, and the list can go on. Yet I find happy people with these conditions all the time. In the middle of a crisis, it can be very tempting to look where to cast the blame, become bitter, and start hating the world and say, why me? But I, for one, think we are all better served, especially during a crisis, to keep focused on finding a solution. We are better served in just realizing that life happens, and of all the million combination of events that occur around us throughout the day, it is highly possible that some of these events will be detrimental to our desires and some even fatal.

While I was in the hospital, complaining about my paralysis, I would watch the news from time to time. One day, I watched a report talking about St. Jude's hospital and their annual fund-raiser. What I realized was that there were children who were so unhealthy they were not expected to reach puberty. When I thought about how much life they were going to miss, I became real despondent at first. Then I realized that although my condition was not ideal, it was far from death, and I felt gratitude—not gratitude for my condition but for the health I still had. Once I felt that emotion, I was able to get better results from my rehabilitation. Now, as I look at my mood compared to as it was before, I am getting along so much better. Now I look at some of the newly injured patients and some of the older ones also, and I can see how their negative attitudes are hindering their progress, not only in their rehabilitation but also in their lives, relationships, and careers.

I hear stories of what people used to do all the time. I used to be this, I used to be that, and they now feel that due to this additional disability, they can no longer perform as they once did. However, when I bring up suggestions like returning to school or taking up a hobby, I am met with more excuses and complaints. I am wondering why that is. It seems that some people stay in that emotional distress that occurred at the time of their accident and that they now define themselves through their disability. But I have met other folks, some who were born disabled and some who were not, who are leading wonderful lives, are happy with their careers and families, and who come to a realization that life is what you make of it and do not waste their lives away complaining about their situation.

I cannot begin to tell you the danger of self-judgment, but unfortunately, it is something we do all the time. We judge ourselves, we judge others around us, and sometimes it serves us, and sometimes it doesn't. When we are walking down a street late at night and we see a group of youngsters all dressed in similar clothing and looking at us dangerously, we create a judgment about this situation and change our direction to avoid that group—an action that may save our lives. But when we find ourselves lying in a hospital bed, suffering from paralysis or some other major trauma, it is no longer serving of us to start judging and asking questions like "Why me? How did this happen?" Then is the time to ask, "How can I get better?" and "What new skills do I need to learn?" and we can focus on healing and living the rest of our lives—but not just living a life but also living a fulfilling life, one with a career we enjoy, with a family we love, and with relationships that support and charge us.

When we learn to judge ourselves not by what happens to us but by how we handle what happens to us, we then have acquired a major tool in helping us deal with adversity. I see a quotation on the side of a building every day I get on the freeway that reads, "In times of struggle, how we respond is everything." I think that can sum it all up nicely. Now, if you think I am saying that this is easy, you could not be farther from the truth. I know it is extremely difficult. It is easy to blame, complain, and suffer. To step back and search for solutions is probably the hardest thing to do, especially at that particular moment. But it is also the most useful, helpful, and fulfilling. And as always, the choice is yours.

Never Ever Stop Dreaming

What are we? Men, women, fathers, mothers, husbands, wives, citizens, musicians, and the list goes on and on and on. How do we become these? Yes, I know some people who are in areas of their lives that are not their preferred choices. Some are even in their last choice, behind bars. Although there are some who might argue that wherever you end up, be it in jail or otherwise, on some level, you chose to be there. I have no interest in debating that issue at this time. What I am here to discuss is the fact that life happens. I am well aware that the original phrase is a bit more colorful, but it is less accurate. The original implies a purely negative connotation and paints an incorrect picture of the unfolding event. It says that bad things happen to you and at times, you may not have any control over the situation. But the truth is, sometimes good things happen to you also and for no apparent reason. It is just when that occurs, we call it luck. In actuality, it too is just life. Sometimes good things come our way; sometimes bad things do. However, we still have a choice. We can define ourselves by what happens to us, or we can define ourselves by what we choose to be.

At some point in our childhoods, I believe we all stated what we wanted to be when we grew up. I submit that the ones who say they are the happiest are the ones who are doing what they always wanted to do. Is that to say they were lucky and we were not? You may be surprised to know that many of the people you now see as famous and lucky were, at one point, more destitute than you or me. Just off the top of my head, I can think of people like Sylvester Stallone and Garth Brooks who each said that while trying to get their careers off the ground, they actually ended up homeless. I remember Harrison Ford saying how he worked long hours as a carpenter while going to and from auditions for acting roles. And then, there are folks like Christopher Reeve. He was born into a reasonably wealthy family; attended private schools then Cornell University; and joined the theater companies; traveled around the country, acting; then attended Juilliard, one of the foremost acting schools in the country. Having Robin Williams as a roommate, Katherine Hepburn as a mentor, John Houseman (from the *Paper Chase*) as a school principal, then getting a job right out of college on a soap opera for $14,000/week, all *before* becoming Superman on the big screen, do seem like a charmed life. Then, all of a sudden, Christopher Reeve is a C2 quadriplegic. I can't begin to tell you what type of internal struggle he had, but just as he was a champion of men before the accident, he became a champion of paralyzed people after it. He stayed who he was and remained true to his dream of acting and being in stage and film. He even acted and directed TV and film *after* his accident.

One man who dreamed of being the president of the United States did not let polio, the disease he was stricken with, stop him from becoming one of the most famous presidents of this country. I am, of course, talking about Franklin D. Roosevelt. As I look around the disabled community, I can see doctors, lawyers, counselors, actors, directors, writers, athletes, husbands, fathers, and leaders. I cannot see any reason why we cannot be what we always wanted to be. Now, I know there will be some exceptions. For example, I know a paralyzed former fighter pilot. I get that. My friend will never fly a military jet again. But does that have to mean he will never fly, period? I am not so sure. But then again, he may no longer want to.

When I was undergoing my rehabilitation course, I had a lot of time to think. One of the subjects that occupied my mind was the future. I had spent most of my life getting ready for one type of career. It didn't even matter what it was anymore because while I was getting accustomed to my new life, I found I no longer desired my old one. I still had dreams, though; they were just different ones. I think the key here is to recognize the difference between chasing a new dream versus giving up on an old one. You see, we are all a summation of our dreams, our aspirations. If we aspire to be a bitter disabled person, we can certainly be that. But if we aspire to be something more, a business person, lawyer, doctor, husband, wife, father, and mother, it is imperative that we all believe that is still possible.

There are a million quotations given by people to inspire us to chase our dreams, but one of my favorites is from Sammy Davis Jr. It reads, "It's not who we are that counts, it's who we want to be." I think he is saying we are who we dream we want to be. Of course, a dream means nothing if there is not any action behind it. This leads me to my second favorite quotation: "A man's reach must extend beyond his grasp, else what's a heaven for?" Without dreams, we could have easily been living in caves, eating whatever we could kill with our homemade spears. OK, maybe that is a little far-fetched now that I look at it, but without dreams and without people chasing them to fruition, the world would be a much more boring place.

So I beseech you. When you are faced with adversity on any level, yes, deal with it. Find a way to cope with it, put some real support in your corner, find happiness at the break of dawn, don't let depression take hold of you, find humor in life, take time to play, get back out into the world, and for God's sake, never *ever* give up on your dreams. Find another if you wish, but chase it, believe in it, and become it. Whether crutches or walker or wheelchair, do not let *anything* keep you from chasing your dream. For the world needs you as much as you need the world.

Love Is Not the Answer, but It May Be the Key

I have spent a lot of time thinking about my (not so) recent experience and wondering how I was able to recover, at least mentally, while so many people in this condition have not. I came to my conclusion by taking a simple inventory of what I (and other success stories) have versus what many others have not. It is not the care, for we are all pretty much equal in that regard. It is not the cause of the accident, for there are as many reasons for paralysis as there are injured people. It is not money because I've watched some injured people with a lot of it simply throw it away on drugs and alcohol. It has nothing to do with a living situation since I've encountered folks that own their own homes, looking and sometimes smelling worse than many of our nation's homeless. At first I deduced that it was hope, that some of the injured folks had it while others did not. And while that did give me some of the answers I needed, I still found this answer to be incomplete. What I finally figured out, the difference between those that fully recover and lead lives with purpose and those that just wander through this life aimlessly—and are sometimes bitter, angry, and sad—was one component. And that component was love.

Love can manifest itself in many different ways. It can be love from a wife, and it can be love from family, friends, or even from strangers. Then I wondered why was it that I had so much love in my life while others had so little? I mean, my girlfriend (now my wife) was by my side usually five out of the seven days of the week. Every week, my father flew out from the other side of the country, and he spent many weeks by my side. When he was there, he was there all day and late into the evening, offering either support or encouragement every step of the way. Other members of my family took significant time to be with me in the hospital during the early crucial days while others were able to check on me constantly for the long haul. Some really close friends traversed long distances to visit me in the hospital, letting me know that their love was there too. One major difference for me than for patients from years past was that I had a cell phone and a laptop computer (provided by the VA hospital). That alone gave me access to something that patients only recently had access to—Facebook. It was only through Facebook that *all* my friends were able to be aware of my experience and send well wishes and converse with me.

So what I discovered was, love did not exist solely by chance. I remember being accused by a good friend many years ago of being in love with the concept of love. Although that is simplifying my feelings toward the subject, I can see the point. Actually, I do believe that not only is love important but it is also the foundation of all that is. It is what we are all searching for, longing to give and receive, and hoping will manifest in our lives somehow. It makes us aspire and achieve more than we could ever do alone, and it can bring us down to levels we would never dream of existing, had we not had a broken heart. To paraphrase, it is only through the course of love that a man's reach may extend beyond his grasp. Else, what's a heaven for?

There have been studies performed on patients with equal situations and medications, and one group was prayed for by a group of friends, family, and strangers, and one was not. The group that was prayed for showed a significantly higher level of recovery than the group that was not. Putting aside whatever personal beliefs you may have for the moment, we can all agree that the group that was prayed for had experienced the effect of love much stronger than the group without the prayer. The source of that love may be debated in another essay, but at least, it came from the people performing the effort of prayer.

Love is not only the great healer, the great supporter, the great initiator, and the great comforter. You could say that without love, the human race would no longer exist. Maybe I realized this many years ago, watching my parents fail at it. Not only mine but also at least 50 percent of the married couples in this country cannot seem to maintain their love and commitment toward each other. What is the secret? I am not sure there is one. My experience is simply never to give up on it. Yes, I have loved some ladies in my lifetime, and many of those relationships did not work out. But I do not think that is a bad thing since I remember them all and learned more about myself and what I wanted in a relationship. It was when I was ready to settle down when I met Sonia, which brings to mind a simple point. I looked for different qualities in a mate when I was looking for a potential wife than when I was looking for just a girlfriend. It may stand to reason why so many relationships fail these days.

So my point of advice here is, when you find yourself ready to settle down, if you are presently in a relationship, you should break up with that person immediately. I know this may sound crazy, but remember, when you asked her out, you were looking for a girlfriend. Now that you are ready for a wife, you should change your criteria in a mate, thus, changing who you would pick to be with. Am I saying that is the answer? No. Is love the be-all and end-all of all that is? No. But maybe, just maybe, like it is in my life, love is the key to learning, understanding, enjoying, and fighting for one's life.

I believe a good portion of my recovery was due to having a reason to wake up in the morning, having a reason to heal and leave the hospital, and having a woman who was waiting and fighting along beside me, helping me heal, holding me when I became frustrated and angry, making sure I ate right and took my medicines and vitamins, and telling me how much she loved me each and every day. Without love, I could have ended up angry, bitter, and miserable. With her love, I am hopeful, excited, and looking toward the future, a future I will be spending with Sonia, my most wonderful wife, standing by my side, just where she has always been since that horrible day I woke up paralyzed in the hospital.

Those out there going through an amazing trial right now, I implore you to seek out the sources of love in your life, the sources of receiving love, and the reasons you give it. Find your own reasons for waking up in the morning, the reasons you hold on to those last minutes before saying good-bye to that special someone, and make those your points of focus during those moments when you think you cannot go on any further. When you are at that point of despair and you are giving yourself reasons for checking out, remember that reason you got up that morning, that reason you are fighting for recovery, and let that fuel you on, give you purpose, and give you hope. That is the true power of love. And if you can surrender to it and allow it inside you, it can be an ally with a power that is immeasurable beyond words.

Stop and Smell the Roses

This is a phrase you often hear but, maybe, are not quite sure that you understand. It does not mean to stop and actually smell roses each time you see them although that practice couldn't hurt. What it means to me is that in spite of all the trials and adversity the world may seem to throw at you, it also provides beauty and serenity. But it is up to you to notice it. You will find it is out there, but so many people just pass it by, all the while complaining about how awful the world is with all the crime, violence, and poverty. I am not saying that crime, violence, and poverty do not exist, but so do love, support, and abundance. In many instances, the negativity out there seems impossible to avoid, and in many instances, that may be true. What must be done in that instance is for us to seek out an example demonstrating love and support of our fellow man.

Our hearts will eventually become attuned to the beauty of the world, and that beauty will begin to dominate our very existence. Wheelchair, crutch, or prosthetic—we are fully capable of becoming a source of light for the world instead of a source of darkness. But first, we need to cultivate that light within us, and it is so much easier than you might think. There is a saying, "You will become what you think about most." So think about the good in the world and acknowledge the bad when you have no other choice, but focus on the good, not just on the good that is done for you but also on the good that is done by you.

This is simply a writing of the lyrics of one of the songs that get me through the day. It is by Mac Davis, a country music singer and all-around good guy.

Hey there, mister, where you goin' in such a hurry?

Don't you think it's time you realized?

There's a whole lot more to life than work and worry.

And the sweetest things in life are free, and they're right before your eyes.

Here I must caution you again. To simply look at the book and jump to rule number ten is an impossible task. Early in your course of rehabilitation, you will be experiencing a whirlwind of emotions that will not allow you to simply relax and take a step back so to speak. Without any type of self—acknowledgement, a friend in your corner, an attitude of happiness from nothing and so forth, you will not be able to see any roses, let alone smell any. Remember, this is a process and a journey, and it needs to be taken one step at a time. Just like undergoing a long journey, it all begins with one single step. This journey however, will be the rest of your life. I still find reasons to look back at my list and remind myself to take time to play, keep focused on my dream, and to keep smelling the roses. This is not a one—time fix all formula, but a lifetime chart and guide of maintaining happiness during this time of major change in your life.

Songs of Engagement

I frequently get asked, "Do you have all your laws memorized?" The answer to that question is no. When I get asked if I carry my laws with me all the time, the answer to that question is yes. There is a special section in my planner for my personal long-term goals, and the rules of engagement are the complete first page. But that is not the only way I try to remember them. I also have chosen one particular song that exemplifies the meaning of each rule, and I have placed them in my MP3 and YouTube listing in order to energize me whenever I am feeling down, tired, and basically have had it for the day, then I look at the clock and it is still four hours until bowel care, or I am in the middle of writing a fifteen-page paper for school and I ask myself, "Why am I punishing myself again?" I have been asked to share the list, and I am happy to do it; however, I urge you to place your song for each rule and make the emotion your own as you go throughout the day.

For rule number one, "You are your first line of defense," my song is "Philadelphia Freedom" by Elton John. Since rule one is about drawing a line in the sand, so to speak, and taking control of yourself and your future, I wanted a song that I know would energize me. For number two, "Put someone in your corner who will not let you fail," I chose the song "Stand By Me." There is the original, and there is a version by a group called Playing for Change. With either version, the message still comes through. For rule number three, "Learn to be happy with nothing," I used a song called "Everything I Need" by Keb' Mo'.

Rule number four is "Depression? OK, but don't let it rule over you forever." This is a special case since depression is not something that just pops up. I also chose the song "Sad Songs (Say So Much)" because it doesn't try to tell you how to get out of the depression but allows you a moment to believe someone out there is feeling the same. "Life goes on, with or without you" is my fifth rule, and the accompanying song to that is "Better Man," again by Keb' Mo'. To this day, I can't listen to this song without keeping my eyes dry. Rule number six is "Every day, take time to play." The song I have chosen for this rule is "One Bad Apple" by the Osmond Brothers, not just for the lyrics—which state basically, just because you've been hurt once, don't give up on living—but also because one of the brothers, Alan to be specific, suffers from MS, and I feel a certain affinity with the family when I listen to their music.

To not measure yourself by what happens to you is basically to accept and embrace change in your life. I realize not every change is desired or even wanted. However, that is the message of the rule; learn that life is change, and there are times when we cannot do anything about it, except roll with it and keep going. That's why I have chosen this song "Time to Change" by the Brady Bunch. Yes, you've read correctly. You can also find the song on YouTube, and I listen to it frequently, not to be cool but to hear the words and find strength and comfort in them.

For the rule "Never ever stop dreaming," I use the song "Keep the Faith" by Michael Jackson—not one of the more popular ones, but for me, hearing Michael say "Don't give up, keep trudging ahead" provides me sometimes with just the right amount of energy I need to get through the rest of the day. And for "Love may be the key," I chose "Beautiful in My Eyes" by Joshua Kadison, but especially on this song, choose the one that truly touches your heart. I've been told by some folks that there is no song out there that touches their heart, and right now, that could be very true. Sometimes the challenge is allowing someone or something to reach your heart. And hey, if it was easy, everyone would have done it already.

Lastly, it's time to "stop and smell the roses." A song you will find by that same name is by a singer called Mac Davis. I urge you to listen first to all these songs and keep the ones that work for you and switch out the ones that do not. Either way, take my song list and make it your own, and use it on those days when you find you need just a bit more energy to make it than you thought you would. It might get you through the evening routine and finally into bed for the night.

Thoughts to Ponder

Whenever we suffer a loss, there may or may not be counseling services available. We must remember, however, there are varying degrees of counselors out there. Some may truly wish to help, some may just be fulfilling a job requirement, and others may have just barely passed their classes in school. Unfortunately, I am one who believes in proper study, especially if you want to try to give me advice that affects my life and my future. My rules of engagement are not rules but suggestions that worked for me when I was facing despair and wondering if I was even going to have a future. One thing is for certain, though—these steps must be taken in the order I have presented them. For example, it matters not if you have someone in your corner if you have not taken any responsibility for your position in life. You will just be wasting the breath and energy of your best friend or closest family member. And you can never accept that life continues on without you while you are still in a state of depression. And you can never overcome your depression until you understand the concept of being happy with nothing.

Everything occurs in steps. Recovery progresses one step at a time, and there is no rushing it. You may have already mastered one of these steps prior to your injury, so during this time, I would ask you to simply remember those life skills while you are in your course of rehabilitation. But remember, the longer you wait to get back on your feet, the harder it will become to do. The mind just doesn't heal itself, and change takes effort and time. But no matter how dark these times may be, please remember the most important lesson I learned during my experience—that even after the longest and harshest of winters, there still arrives spring.

Issues of Comorbidity

Comorbidity basically means "a condition that exists simultaneously and independently of another condition." By now, you are well aware that along with your paralysis, you are dealing with issues of bowel and bladder management and skin-ulcer dangers. Or along with your amputation, you are finding issues of balance and coordination. Maybe you are recovering from a mastectomy, and you have concerns regarding a resurgence of the cancer you are battling. Either way, the condition you are now dealing with has had more than one ramification. Your life has now changed on more than one area. Your physical regimen has been modified to increase your arm strength to allow your arms to become your primary means of locomotion. This will be accompanied by sore elbows and shoulders and, more than likely, injuries to those same body parts. You will need to adjust to a new method of locomotion. The difficult part is, of course, having to cope with so many other issues that you did not have before.

Now you are ready to learn one last concept: loss is change, and change involves loss. It doesn't really matter if you are switching high schools or limbs. Each requires a skill in coping with change. Life requires change in order to grow. You may not feel that this particular situation is growth, but it may help if you think of it as forced growth. Here, you can either grow or be stuck in the reactive, emotional state of your injury for years. But I don't have any overly used clichés here, and time does not heal all wounds, nor can you just move beyond this. At best, you can make this an acceptable part of who you are while not allowing it to define who you are. In other words, just because you have a prosthetic leg does not make you a crippled person. Only if you allow this prosthetic limb to affect your future outcome in any way are you succumbing to the limb.

I guess the purpose of this chapter is self-management. Yes, you will be burdened with other issues besides your injury. Just as you learned how to manage your injury, you will learn to manage your bowel, bladder, arms, and shoulders. You will learn how to field questions regarding your injury, and you will work your way back into regular life. You will go shopping for food, clothing, furniture, and anything else you will need to continue on with life. You will find friends to replace the ones that are no longer around, and you will find love if you do not already have one. I know many paraplegics, male and female, who have found their present spouse after their accident. They have children, jobs, and relationships that are just as fulfilling as anyone's. I am not telling you this in an attempt to frame your reality or emotions. My hope, though, is to relieve you of any fear or uncertainty that may be enveloping you. No matter how confident you may be feeling now, you may experience a feeling of uncertainty as your discharge date comes closer. Please realize you only need to take things one day at a time, and remember how to put first things first. Your priorities will have to change, but that does not need to be a painful process.

In my situation, I needed to understand that I have to set my alarm clock to awaken me every four hours during the evening. I use a method known as intermittent catheterization (IC) to manage my bladder. Basically, what that means is, I have to use a catheter every four hours to urinate. There is no getting around this unless I do not drink any water, which is very unhealthy for my kidneys. So I plan my day on when I have to perform an IC. For example, if we are at a friend's home and it is getting time to leave, I make sure I can perform an IC before I get into the car. And if my friend does not have a bathroom that can accommodate my wheelchair, I arrange to IC beforehand, but I have to leave before I have to perform another one. Otherwise, I will end up having an accident in my pants, which I do not want. This also means that when I go to bed for the evening, I must set my alarm so I can wake up in the middle of the night and perform an IC then switch positions and go back to sleep for another four hours.

At first I found it frustrating and bothersome, and sometimes I would sleep through the alarm and wake up in a soaking wet bed. These mornings were not fun in the least. Now I don't try to fight the situation; I just acknowledge my new priority and understand that nothing can happen until my bladder-management situation is resolved. Eventually, you will get to this point and find that life is still enjoyable.

Life After Spinal Cord Injury

OK, so you've already awakened in your hospital room without the use of your legs, arms, or maybe a limb was amputated and you no longer have a limb altogether. You have healed from your injuries, completed your intensive program of rehabilitation, modified your home to accommodate your condition, and met with your vocational rehabilitation counselor to discuss your future. The question is, "What now?" The reason I say that is because that is exactly the same process I went through. During my rehabilitation, I was asked many times what modifications I would need to implement at my job so I could continue on with my duties. The question I should have been asked is if I desired to return to my previous duties.

I appreciate the military's and the VA's efforts to provide funding for veterans to attend school, and there are many programs available. However, I was a veteran who served prior to September 11, 2001, and I had already used my GI Bill over ten years ago, and my injuries were not considered service connected. I had to seek out other avenues.

As I was discussing my predicament with my kinesiotherapist (KT), he mentioned a program called Swim with Mike. I did some research and found out some incredible information. In 1981, Mike Nyeholt, a three-time all-American USC swimmer, became paralyzed in a motorcycle accident. A fund-raiser was organized in order to provide Mike with a specially equipped van for his transportation. There was an excess of funds raised, so at Mike's suggestion, the remainder of the funds was distributed to other disabled individuals who were attempting to return to school. The following year, Mike's teammate Ron Orr (now the senior associate athletic director at USC) created "Swim with Mike" where Mike Nyeholt returned to the campus to swim laps in order to continue to raise money for disabled people attempting to return to school. Now, Mike swims laps at various locations over the country, including Hawaii, and has, to date, over five hundred participants.

"To not be able to play the sport you love can be devastating, but my friend Ron Orr started 'Swim with Mike' to prove there is a support system to moving on, especially when it comes to education," said Nyeholt.

I further learned that although this program is funded from USC, there are only seven students enrolled at USC while there are forty-two students enrolled at universities and colleges throughout the United States. In order to qualify for this scholarship, the applicant must have participated in an organized sports program at the high school or collegiate level and suffered an illness or injury that results in a life-limiting physical disability. The applicant must also meet the attending university's admission requirements and maintain a 2.5 GPA while enrolled in the program. After learning about this program, I decided to apply.

I am proud to announce that I will be attending USC in the fall of 2012, and without the assistance of Swim with Mike, I am not sure that this would be possible. My life has opened in ways that I could have never even dreamed of since the day I was discharged from the hospital. I remember feeling so alone. Then I learned there were people before me who had suffered and overcome similar accidents and illnesses, and they had paved a path for me to follow, if only I could overcome my paralyzing fear and venture upon it. And now, two years later, it is I inviting you to venture out; realize life is not over and that a new beginning awaits if you are ready to move forward. All you need to do is discover your new passion, discuss with your counselor the appropriate major needed to fulfill it, request an application from USC or your desired university or college, download an application from www.swimwithmike.org, and start on the path toward your new life. And maybe one day, you too will "swim with Mike."

So you see—or hopefully will soon see—that your life is not over. In fact, it is just beginning. You still have plenty of choices open to you, whether your accident occurred during your youth, middle years, or senior years. Life is change, change is life, and all life is precious.

Author Bio

Scoba Rhodes was born in Falmouth, Massachusetts, in 1966. He graduated from Bowdoin College in 1987, earned an honorable discharge from the US Navy in 1994, and is currently striving for a master's degree from the University of Southern California. In November 2009 he went in for a procedure to repair an abdominal aortic aneurysm and awoke paralyzed from the waist down, forced to live out the remainder of his life as a T-10 complete paraplegic. After serving in the navy—where he was selected as a battle station reactor operator and quality assurance supervisor, earning the Southwest Asia Medal for his service in Desert Shield/Desert Storm and an Admiral's Commendation for his outstanding service—he underwent successful stints in direct sales, advertising, and logistics. When he was injured, he spent almost a year in the hospital, healing and rehabilitating and wondering what was going to happen with the rest of his life. One day, after he had dropped 115 pounds and was dangerously underweight, his wife pleaded with him to stop wasting his life and get back to being the man that she initially fell in love with. He then began a personal journey back from the depths of depression and restored the vibrant, successful, fulfilling life that existed before the accident.

CPSIA information can be obtained at www.ICGtesting.com
Printed in the USA
LVOW13*0700260514

387278LV00002B/27/P